Title Page

Tools for Lifelong Learning about Living Well

First Edition

© Copyright 2018, John Patrick Gatton and Jenna Marie Gilman

To email the authors visit the website:
successinlivinglifewell.org

About the Authors

John Patrick Gatton

For eighteen years as an independent management consultant, I advised and trained executives of national American corporations in how to create and sustain a motivational work environment, and how to become successful national consultants.

I have conducted workshops with hundreds of people who have cancer, and, also for Family Caregivers. I have recently published a related book, *God's Strengthening Love For Caregivers*. Also published is a personally narrated CD titled, *Stories That Ignite Healing*.

I twice completed the Ignatian Spiritual Exercises with Fr. Joe Neville at the Loyola Jesuit Center in Morristown NJ. Fr. Joe's example and the exercises are powerful, perpetual influencers in my life. This book is blended with Christian beliefs.

Relevant Information

Naval Aviator, United States Navy. Patrol Plane Commander, VP 16
Graduate with Bachelor of Science from the University of Illinois

Various corporate positions including Director, Employee and Labor Relations,
Director Organization Planning
Creator of expert systems for collecting and summarizing customer satisfaction data
Successful twenty seven year recovery from cancer and its remedies
Creator of seminars for helping people with cancer, and for family caregivers to heal and succeed in their very complex life situations

Jenna Marie

Jenna Marie is a contributing writer to this book. She also assisted with editing, and she commented on the content and organization of the manuscript as it was in process. Jenna Marie is a graduate of Stonehill College and is pursuing advanced degrees in Nursing with a specialty in Mental Health. She has an intuitive understanding of motivational environments.

What this book is about
Why You Should Read this Book

The tools, stories, and writings in this book can enable individuals, families, and discussion groups to achieve lifelong success in adjusting to major life events. It provides a concise common language of proven tools and skills development exercises for adjusting to life's changing cycles. Suggestions for building and maintaining positive personal and group living environments are easy to use. Twenty-eight uplifting stories, and writings by the authors stimulate the building of positive living skills.

A personal note:

This book is developed by a family team, Grandfather Patrick Gatton, and Granddaughter Jenna Marie. I am certain that Jenna's future editions of this book will be valued by those who need broad-based practical methods to help them live well as they experience life's ever-changing challenges and its natural cycles.

John Patrick Gatton

Dedication:

This book is dedicated to all of the hundreds of folks who, during my directed seminars, workshops, and retreats across America have asked insightful questions and shared their wisdom about how to live well. They have benefited me by sharing their lives, their circumstances, and knowledge that comes simply by living life's complex experiences.

It is also dedicated to those who will benefit from the ever-developing education, experience and sharing of the wisdom of many folks as Jenna Marie writes about events related to her life purpose of helping others heal.

Chapter One - Tool Number One
Discovering What To Do Now

Motivational environments and indicators of living well

About Living Well

Living well includes sharing life stories about maturing, listening to how others are handling life situations, successful recovery from tough situations, sharing fun and wisdom gained through experience, building our skills to enjoy life, and experiencing an occasional positively thrilling moment. A moment such as a grand slam in baseball, or a grand slam in the card game called Bridge.

This book is designed to help you understand readily available tools, and processes for developing skills of living well. It focuses on learning a commonly shared and concise language that stimulates conversations about how to enjoy life. This book presents opportunities to know about what you need to do to live well.

Each of us contributes to our daily living environment. The materials in this book focus on the qualities of a positive living environment and how we contribute to that positive living environment. It also focuses on essential tools and skills development for enjoying life and contributing to an enjoyable family experience, social group experiences, and your community's living environment.

It is important to learn about how we are affecting our own lives and the lives of others through our daily decisions and activities. The tools presented in this book assist in your search for what to do now. The stories and writings are designed to help you decide that living well in all of life's cycles is achievable. The writings also provide insights about how our own behavior affects the feelings and the lives of our families, our neighbors, and our community living.

———

Learning Opportunity:
Read and consider the following eight selected consistent qualities of a motivational living environment.

———

Eight Qualities of a Motivational Living Environment

1. Members of the family, social groups, and communities are aware of the value of each person as a contributing member of a family, a group, and a community.
2. Members make casual and formal expressions of appreciation of the contributions others make to the family, the group, and the community.
3. Members frequently demonstrate confidence in individual members with the intent to encourage self-esteem.
4. Individuals accept personal responsibility for their own well being and their contribution to the larger group.
5. An updated simple plan of action exists to provide guidance in reacting to and managing the evolving challenges occurring today, this week, and this month.

6. Individuals are involved in activities that promote physical, mental, emotional, and spiritual health and wellbeing.
7. Members are continually updating their awareness of any personal need for help in living well, and they accept the help offered by others who are credible.
8. Continual learning and skills development in the use of tools that encourage involvement in events that are healthy, that create the feeling of satisfaction associated with achievement, that stimulate self esteem and produce an occasional positively uplifting moment in daily life.

———

Learning Opportunity:
You are now familiar with eight consistent qualities of a positive living environment. Congratulations!

———

Becoming Familiar With
Fourteen Selected Indicators about living well

Learning Opportunity:
The purpose of the exercises on the next pages is to familiarize you with fourteen selected indicators of living well and enable you to know what you can do to feel better.
1. Go to the completed survey below, read and take note of the <u>underlined responses</u>.
2. After reading and noting the example responses, answer the two questions following the completed survey.

A Completed Survey Example
Learn by noting and considering the underlined responses on this completed survey of fourteen selected Indicators of living well.

How much have you been doing in the past year?

	Little	Some	Much		
1. Socializing with friends and acquaintances	1	2	**3**	4	5
2. Recognizing my contributions to others	1	2	**3**	4	5
3. Balancing the activities on my schedule	1	**2**	3	4	5
4. Forgiving those who cause my hurts	**1**	2	3	4	5

How much have you been doing in the past year?

	Little		Some		Much
5. Using meditation or contemplation to gain strength	1	2	3	**4**	5
6. Controlling my finances	1	2	3	4	**5**
7. Physical exercising	1	2	3	**4**	5
8. Eating healthy foods	1	2	3	**4**	5
9. Nurturing a relationship with a confidant	1	**2**	3	4	5
10. Asking God to help in my life events	1	**2**	3	4	5
11. Creating laughter	1	**2**	3	4	5
12. Inviting laughter into my life	**1**	2	3	4	5
13. Persistently maintaining positive thoughts	1	2	**3**	4	5
14. Examining and updating my assumptions	1	**2**	3	4	5

_____

Learning Opportunity:
After reading and considering the underlined responses in the above sample survey, answer the following two questions:
1. If the completed example were your own personal profile, which of the indicators would you select as most important for you to now take action to gain the benefits of living well?
2. Why?

―――――

Learning Opportunity:
The purpose of the next exercise is to help you recognize, consider, and mark the selected fourteen indicators of living well. Thoughtful consideration of how much you are doing now, as indicated by your response to each indicator, will help you to identify what is important for you to do now, and then develop a simple plan that promotes living well.

Read the fourteen indicators listed on the next pages and circle your response 1-5 for each indicator. Then, you can develop a plan of things to do to feel better and continually succeed while experiencing life's cycles.

First Step: Respond to the fourteen selected Indicators of opportunities to live life well by circling your response on the scale of 1-5.

<u>SecondStep</u>: Review your responses and determine which indicator is most important to you at this time.

_____

Read and complete following survey by circling your responses 1-5 to each indicator.

Your Personal Survey: 14 Indicators of Living Well

How much have you been doing in the past year?

	Little		Some		Much
1. Socializing with friends and acquaintances	1	2	3	4	5
2. Recognizing my contributions to others	1	2	3	4	5
3. Balancing the activities on my schedule	1	2	3	4	5
4. Forgiving those who cause me to hurt	1	2	3	4	5
5. Using contemplation or meditation to gain strength	1	2	3	4	5
6. Controlling my finances	1	2	3	4	5
7. Physical exercising	1	2	3	4	5

8. Eating healthy foods   1   2   3   4   5

9. Nurturing a relationship
   with a confidant   1   2   3   4   5

10. Asking God to help me in
    my life events   1   2   3   4   5

11. Creating laughter   1   2   3   4   5

12. Inviting laughter into my life   1   2   3   4   5

13. Persistently maintaining
    positive thoughts   1   2   3   4   5

14. Reviewing and updating
    my assumptions   1   2   3   4   5

———

Learning Opportunity:
Observe your marked responses to the survey of the
selected indicators above. Discover and select the most
important indicator for you to begin gaining the benefits
of using the eight tools described in this book. Repeat
this process often to stay current on what needs to be
done now to help you to persistently live well.

Chapter Two - Tool Number Two
Uplifting Messages and Humor

Note: If you read the following stories aloud, your fuller concentration will make them more meaningful.

Let's Examine Humor
A Story about Humor

I wanted to know how I could add to the humor and laughter that uplifts the human spirit. So, I climbed the Mountain of Humor to get the full view of humorous thought. Arriving at the summit of Humor Mountain, I met the master teacher of life-enriching humor. In bold surprise, I said, *Please teach me how to create humor.*

Each person is gifted to create harmony in life, said the teacher. *Humor creates laughter and harmony among us. Humor is an essential ingredient of harmony.*

I asked, *How do I learn to create such humor? First, learn to laugh at yourself,* said the teacher as we chatted there at the peak of Humor Mountain. *When you perfect that skill, laughter will follow. Then return to me and I will teach you how to help others do the same.*

———

A story
A Speed Dating Conversation at Age Eighty Three

Bill: If I were your age and single, I would go to Italy.
Jill: That is also what I would like to do. However, I have the same number of years that you have.
Bill: That is hard for me to believe. Where would you go in Italy?
Jill: I would go directly to a villa in the mountains.

Bill: What would you do there?
Jill: I would stay in the villa, walk in the gardens, eat the grapes, sit in the sun, drink a glass of wine and sleep in the shade. If you went to Italy, where would you go?

Bill: I would book the same flight as you, the same villa as you, walk in the gardens, drink the wine of the local vine, sit in the sun, and rest in the shade.

Bill: Shall we dance?
Jill: Yes.

Bill: Shall we dine together?
Jill: Yes.

Jill: Shall we book a trip to Italy?
Bill: Maybe next year.

Jill: Want to sit in the shade?
Bill: Only until we are ready to dance again.

Jill: It is good to know someone of my age who has such energy.

———

A Laugh Is a Prayer

Your smile is pleasing to each you greet, your face lights, you chuckle then raise your eyes in surprise. Your reaction to a fantastic story showers amusement over your companions. Why, you even delete a comma with flare.

You wander to and from standard expectations with delight. You like being with agreeable folks who giggle, articulate humor and gift the court jester. Your relaxed face creates an invitation to fun-filled subjects that create stretching smiles, bright eyes, and splendid guffaws.

Our delight is in watching your face as your breath bursts forth and seriousness heads north to the land of silence. It is delightful to believe that your laughter charms the Creator of you and us, and all that is.

———

Laughter Is Good for Our Health

Try this following exercise while taking time out to laugh:

Learning Opportunity:
1. Schedule a time in your day to spend one minute laughing. Laugh as you like for one full moment. During each week, extend the time of your laughing

until you are occasionally laughing for a full five minutes. 😊

2. When you notice you are frustrated, up tight, or tense, change your mood by recognizing your state of tension; then laugh for fifteen-seconds. 😆

3. Laugh for ten-seconds when you get up, before meals, after you watch the news, when someone steps in the line in front of you, and when you go to bed.

———

Giggling

It starts with a thought, or a silly boy who slipped and broke a floppy toy. Way down in your belly a giggle begins, you try to hold back but it always wins.

It's so much fun to giggle with the other kids, especially when grown-ups don't know why. Don't you just love to giggle until you cry? Why is a giggle so contagious? Perhaps it's just that what we see really is outrageous, and nobody else knows.

———

Recognizing Physical Stress
Awareness and relaxation techniques

It is healthy to recognize when we are physically 😐 stressed.

Learning to recognize that our body is tense enables us to be aware of that tension. Then we can use physical exercise, meditation or contemplation imagery, and laughter to relax our mental, physical, and emotional state. Relaxing boosts our feeling of well-being.

Learning Opportunity:
Use the following exercise to become aware when your muscles are tense or tightened.

Exercise: In a sitting position: tighten all the body's muscles and hold for 10 seconds (or so) and then relax all muscles in the body. Repeat this exercise up to five times.

Let yourself record and remember the difference in your feelings with tightened muscles and when your muscles are relaxed.

Do one of the following:
1. Use the meditation/contemplation process to help you relax. Page 38
2. Do physical exercise to help you relax.
3. Laugh out loud 😆 for fifteen-seconds (or more) to help you change your focus to relaxation and happiness.

———

Learning Opportunity:

Consider, and discuss the following confirming statements that may awaken you to new possibilities in your daily activities:

1. I know the process for recognizing physical stress.
2. I am able to recognize stress within me.
3. I will continue developing my skills of recognizing physical stress and using simple methods to relax.

When you have relaxed, use the following learning opportunity to stimulate your thinking about sharing, hoping, reaching out, and being cheerful.

<u>Learning Opportunity:</u>
Consider and respond to the following statements

Living Well includes:

	Yes	No
• The sharing of love	—	—
• Being hope-filled	—	—
• Reaching out to help others	—	—
• Enjoying being cheerful	—	—

_____

How do you feel?   A+

Chapter Three - Tool Number Three
Assuming Equality

Our assumptions about being equal to others do matter.

Some Motivational Effects of Assuming Equality

Objective: To help you consider the importance of accepting your own equality with all people.

Thinking of ourselves as being equal to other people helps us to reach out and engage in healthy activities with positive thinking people and groups. This assumption promotes the tendency to continually seek motivational community environments and to create a personal motivational living environment for ourselves.

Learning Opportunity:
Expanding our understanding of an assumption and how an assumption affects our thinking.

Definition: The word assumption is a noun. A common definition is - a *thing that is accepted as true without proof.*

Commonly accepted synonyms of the word, assumption include - a thought, an expectation, a speculation, a belief, a supposition, a guess, a surmise, a premise.

Method of Learning - read the following three stories, search for, discover, and list the author's assumptions. Compare his assumptions to your own assumptions about being equal to all other people.

_____

A story to stimulate discussion

What If?

What if you and I both assume that we are created equal? Our relationship would be like a partnership and each could enjoy the other's company. What would change in our relationship if each of us changed from assuming that we are created equal to assuming that one of us is less than the other? Friction would develop, or each of us might accept that the other one is either more than I, or lesser than I.

If we both assume that, *I am more than you,* how would our relationship change from what it was when each assumed that both are equal?

Friction would interfere with harmony. Exclusion would become a viable option. Making less of the other person would become a tendency. Separation would become a solution. Conflict would become a justifiable activity.

Perhaps being equal is the better alternative.

_____

The essential message of the next story is, I am equal to all persons.

_____

Equality

Being equal, we are just as nature has made us. Being equal, one has complete respect for self, curiosity about the stories of each person met, and happiness when encountering other people.

Being equal, we can be a companion for a moment or a lifetime. Equality exists when each has an equal position in life, the same justice, the same civil rights, and respect for the gifts of each person.

Effects of equality include encouragement of other people, respect for the talents and skills of each person, and equal votes in all important events. The effects of equality also include experiencing happiness, easy and friendly laughter, independence, freedom, and mutual support.

These effects of equality exist when we have mutual respect for each person without premature judgment, when we have happiness in a meeting with other people, and when we have the desire to contribute to the life experiences of each person. We author equality in this world. We create the benefits of equality in this world. We receive the effects of equality in this world.

———

Learning Opportunity:

About the Value of Being Equal

If we human beings are created as equal, can anyone make another of us less than equal to him or her?

Consider the following two assumptions, then discuss them with those you trust, perhaps a confidant:

1. No matter what one achieves including fame, fortune or sainthood, history shows that one never becomes more that any other human being. One can be more honored for achieving fame, fortune or sainthood, however, one does not become more than other people in terms of being created as equal, being loved and being accepted.

2. Since I am created equal to all other persons, only I can make less of me through my free-will choices.

———

How do you feel?   A+

Chapter Four - Tool Number Four
Declaring a Purpose in Life

Purposes in life stimulate positive activities. Declaring a definite positive purpose in life creates a highly motivational statement that triggers an individual's inner desires to take positive action.

A common definition of the word, motivational, is promoting the willingness or desire to achieve something.

Learning Opportunity:
Spend the time required to think about the primary and secondary current positive purposes in your life and then declare them.

1. I declare that the primary purpose of my life is:

_____

2. I declare that secondary purposes in my life include:

_____

How do you feel?   A+

Chapter Five - Tool Number Five
Updating Our Assumptions

Update an Assumption and You can Change a Life

Note: Becoming aware of and examining our assumptions and how they affect our strength, our feelings, and our achievements is a superb skill to have in times of change.

If one of our assumptions limits our options for living well we can change it to a positive and inclusive assumption. This change of an assumption can result in major changes in one's life, in family life, and in community life. This change can also enhance our personal achievements and success in living well as life's cycles change.

A common definition: The word, assumption, is a noun and is defined - a thing that is accepted as true without proof.

Commonly accepted synonyms of the word assumption include - a thought, an expectation, a speculation, a belief, a supposition, a guess, a surmise, a premise.

Learning Opportunity:
The motivational effects of the words, possible, and, possibility, are worth examining.

The effects of using the word, possible, tends to limit thinking to an already existing situation.

The word, possibility, opens the boundaries of a conversation to include a likelihood of succeeding exists, a hope exists, or there is a probability that something could happen if conditions were changed.

On occasion we ask ourselves, *Is it possible for me, or us, to succeed?* This question may cause us to review current conditions but not trigger an inner motivation to achieve. It tends to limit a review of our present assumptions and restrict thinking to our presently known resources.

The question we should ask is this, *Is there a possibility that I, or we, can achieve success?* This question triggers the opportunity to think differently and ask additional questions like, *What would need to happen for me, or us, to succeed?* Or, *What would have to change for me, or us, to succeed?*

By changing our focus to the second question to, *Is there a possibility?* we trigger the opportunity to examine and change our restrictive assumptions. When we examine and change our restrictive assumptions we promote creative thinking and stimulate discussions about what needs to change and what resources would we need to create the possibility of succeeding.

———

Following is a scale that helps us become aware of our assumptions. This scale is set up to help you answer this question, *Is there a possibility that I, or we, can succeed in living well in the changing cycles of life?*

To answer the question, consider the following scale as it applies to you. Doing so will help you become aware of your assumptions about succeeding in meeting the challenges inherent in life's changing cycles.

Learning Opportunity:
Consider the following question then mark your answer on the following five point scale.

The question: *Is there a possibility that I, or we, can succeed in living well in the changing cycles of life?*

The scale of responses -
1. __ I don't know how that could happen.

2. __ Probably not.

3. __ I, or we, might succeed.

4. __ Success is a possibility if we consider how to change the current situation.

5. __ I am, or we are, succeeding.

_____

Commonly Known Challenges We Encounter
Life's cycles bring different challenges

1. Losses including - reduction of status: reduced achievements; a change of location; less family contact; leaving friends and losing friends; a sense of being less important to family and community.

2. Personal changes including - spiritual; physical; emotional; downsizing; and the importance of our contributions to others.

3. Internal changes Including - awakening to new meanings of life; changes in interests and hobbies; our ability to help others; organizational memberships; wondering where maturing adults fit into family events while younger families are so very active; learning to deal with social changes caused by changing technology. Also, questioning our evolving purpose in life.

———

Learning Opportunity:
Stories that Stimulate Discussion

Read the following three stories, then complete the learning opportunity exercise that follows each of those stories.

———

A story
There Was a Time

There was a time when I focused on results, a time of great concentration, of self confidence, exploring, learning, advancing. I reviewed telephone books for the challenge of memorizing random numbers.

I counted black-eyed salmon in the Hudson River simply to accomplish an impossible task while unfailingly striving to become one of the fantastic achievers in the world.

I have changed and now write stories to create flawed descriptions of possibilities; later going out to complete related tasks with vigor and blemished results. I am a man now tired of perfection, obsession, high-strung motivation, and the hernias created in striving for perfection.

In workshops I am learning the value of imperfect descriptions that blow away the idea of faultlessness and create idyllic perceptions of life's realities. Now, I am a happy man searching each day for ways to imperfectly describe those lesser things I now cherish as golden achievements.

———

Learning Opportunity:
Answer this question - how and why did the man telling the story change during the years of his maturing?

———

Doubt Does Not Exist

Doubt does not exist in perfect love, for it contains only pure truth and confidence. The gift of confidence that comes with perfect love has no grades of perfection and exists without doubt. Perhaps a new possibility is to accept the gift of confidence contained within God's perfect love for me and for you.

_____

Learning Opportunity: - Examining assumptions
1. Search for the authors assumptions in the story, Doubt Does Not Exist.
2. List the assumptions you noted.
3. Examine the assumptions and label each as supportive of positive outcomes that enhance success; or as a supporter of negative outcomes that limit possibilities of living life well.

_____

Set Free

Imagine a lecture that drones endlessly, a stressful day at the office with a to-do list too long for a page, an extended car ride with no means of entertainment. Nearly everyone has to pull themselves back into reality after staring at life through a selected window. We find ourselves looking through a favored window entertaining thoughts and daydreams to distract us from the task at hand.

Literally speaking, windows are openings allowing the passage of light. However, windows serve a far greater purpose; they display an inviting environment, connect us to nature, become passageways to our inner thoughts, wishes and dreams.

Windows flood rooms with sunshine and soft breezes during the day and serve as subtle reminders of a nurturing world outside, while we seem immobile inside our lesser thoughts. Windows are catalysts for sparking our imaginations and escaping the mundane in daily life. The windows we choose for viewing the world can set us free.

Jenna Marie, Author

———

Learning Opportunity:
Examining assumptions

Search for the author's assumptions in the above essay titled - Set Free.
1. List the assumptions you noted.
2. Examine the assumptions and label each as supportive of positive outcomes that enhance success, or as negative outcomes that limit possibilities of living life well.

Chapter SixTool Number Six
Meditation/Contemplation

Common definitions of terms:

1. The term meditation refers to a broad variety of practices that include techniques designed to promote relaxation, build internal energy or life force.

2. Contemplation is profound thinking about something.

A meditation prayer
Guided imagery that helps us relax and heal

Note: This prayer assumes that Jesus is involved in our daily lives.

Practice by reading the following relaxation process to relax and heal until you can do it without reading it:

1. Take 3 deep breaths.

2. Relax. Be comfortable.

3. Let your eyes close.

4. Count down from 5-0 and relax more deeply with each count.

5. Allow yourself to go deeper into relaxation.

6. Visualize a garden with a stream flowing, happy people, beautiful yellow, blue, green flowers. Notice trees so tall you can barely see the tops, and trees so small you could hold one in your hand.

Notice the peaceful presence of light in the garden. This is the light of creation and healing.

7. Enter the garden. When you are ready, notice the flowers, plants, the intense and lovely colors, and

waters, notice all life in the garden is filled with the light of creation and healing.

8. Notice a nearby chair made of flower pedals. Sit in the chair and relax.

9. Notice a woman sitting in the chair close to you. She says, My *name is Mary, hold my hand and let me share peacefulness with you.* Mary tells you that the light contained in this garden is light directly from the presence of Jesus in this garden.

10. Notice the relaxed beauty of Mary's smile promoted by her feeling that she is perfectly loved and perfectly accepted. She exudes peace from within herself.

11. Relax now and hear Mary say, *Let yourself be peaceful, Jesus is here with a gift for you.*

As she tells you of the presence of Jesus, you see Him standing in front of you with His hands over your head.

12. In your relaxed state, allow the light of creation, peace, and healing to flow from the hands of Jesus into the top of your head.

Let the light of creation, peace, and healing flow down into your head, your brain, your ears, your eyes, your throat, your jaw.

Especially, let your jaw relax completely.

13. Notice your breathing may now be deeper, more regular.

14. Imagine the light of creation, healing, and peace flowing down through your shoulders, your elbows, your wrists, down through your fingers.

You might now notice your fingers tingling.

15. Let the light of creation, peace, and healing flow easily through you.

16. Give permission for your cells to release all negative memories.

17. Let the light of love, creation, peace and healing flow down through your chest, stomach, major organs, into your pelvic area, down through your knees, your ankles, your feet, let the light flow through your toes, also pushing out the negative memories to wherever nature sends such memories.

18. You may notice tingling in your toes as negative memories are pushed out by the light of healing.

19. Relax, enjoy the flow of the light of creation, peace, and healing through you. This is the light of love,

creation, peace, and healing. Let this light flow within you.

20. Let all negative memories flow out pushed by the flow of this peaceful and healing light.

21. Now, let's go deeper into relaxation.

22. Relax now. Stay at this relaxed level for a moment. Let yourself remember the steps of this process. You can go to this level of relaxation when you feel tension; tightening muscles.

23. Notice the flow of light, the light of creation, peace, and healing flowing through you. Now, focus that light in the place in your body that needs it most.

24. Now, let your mind focus on a person who needs healing and direct this healing light to flow to him or her for a minute or so.

25. It is now possible that you can become relaxed to this level whenever you decide to relax.

26. Begin now to return to the awareness of this room:
Count up from 0 - 5
Notice the pressure on your seat.
Notice your feet on the floor.
Notice where your hands are.
Hear the sounds in the room.

27. Let your eyes open.

<u>Learning Opportunity</u>:

Answer the following questions:
1. How do you feel? A+
2. What did you experience?
3. What did you observe?

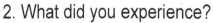

Discovering New Possibilities
through meditation/contemplation

The following three statements can open us to new possibilities in living well through meditation or contemplation.

Consider these confirming statements that may awaken you to new possibilities in your daily activities:
1. The processes of meditating/contemplating create peace within me.

2. I remember the steps of the process so I can use them to easily create peace within myself.

3. I will continue to develop my skill of meditation or contemplation for the purpose of succeeding in living well.

Chapter Seven - Tool Number Seven
Changing a Negative Thought

Changing a Negative Thought to a Positive Thought

Definition: A negative thought is one that produces damaging results.

Negative thoughts are noticeable in most of our lives, sometimes they are random and sometimes they repeat in rapid succession.

For example: The negative thought, *I can't learn to use a cell phone,* might be the title of a thought you become aware of. Because it states that, *I can't learn*, this thought can deter any effort to learn to use a cell phone or can cause failure in attempted learning.

This negative thought may come to you at anytime. It can be changed in a simple five step process.

Five Steps to change a negative thought to a positive thought:

Step: Recognition. Learn to recognize a negative thought as it comes into your mind. Negative thoughts include those of fear, guilt, dread, horror, fright, alarm, panic, insecurity, distress, trepidation, timidity. They are negative thoughts because they produce results that are damaging. (an exception is fear in emergency situations)

Examples: Negative thoughts could begin with words like the following: *I dread, I may not be worthy, I cannot accomplish, I should have, I am afraid of, What if something bad happens? I don't have, I can't, I didn't do (whatever), I did (something) wrong.*

An example of a title of a negative thought is: *Because I have the disease named, (whatever) I fear that (something bad) will happen.*

An example of becoming aware of a negative thought and recognizing it as a negative thought: *Say hello to the thought with a title such as, I fear that something bad will happen. I recognize you as a negative thought.*

Note: This is a direct recognition of the negative thought.

Step: Accept the negative thought.

Example of accepting the negative thought:
Say, *I recognize you as the thought - I fear that something bad will happen, and I accept you.*

Step: Change the Title. Announce to the negative thought that you are now going to change its title. Changing the title of a negative thought to a positive one changes the thought to a positive thought.
Example of changing negative thought to a positive one:
1. Say to the thought titled - *I fear something bad will happen, I recognize and accept you. I am now going to change your title to a positive title that enhances my health.*

2. *Your new title is - The Presence of Jesus.* (tailor this title to meet your needs).

Step: Declare that the change is made and give thanks.
1. Say, *I declare this change is made and you are now a positive thought that enhances my health.*
2. Say, *thanks God for this healing change in my life.*

Acknowledge the thought has Changed: accept the fact that the thought has been changed to match the new positive title. Also, the new title is permanent until again changed by you.

Note: If similar negative thoughts occur, repeat the above five step process.

———

Discovering new possibilities through changing negative thoughts.

Consider the following confirming statements that may awaken you to new possibilities in managing negative thoughts in your daily activities:
1. I understand the process for changing a negative thought to a positive thought.
2. I am able to change a negative thought that comes into my mind.

Chapter Eight - Tool Number Eight
Strengthening Our Positive Thoughts

Strengthening a Positive Thought

Positive thoughts enable us to focus on successful plans and engage in activities that build our skills enabling us to achieve positive goals and objectives. They are important allies in living well in the changing cycles of life.

Positive thoughts are important to healing. Positive thoughts are contagious. When we express positive thoughts to other people, they also feel better.

Positive thoughts have titles that include these examples: *I am good at being a Doctor, Nurse, Teacher, Manager, Craftsperson, Technician, Chauffeur, Minister, Mother, Father, Student, Clerk, Supervisor.*

A positive thought serves a useful purpose in your life such as enabling you to achieve good results. Each positive thought was given its title such as, *I am good at (anything)*, by you sometime in your life.

Most positive thoughts can be strengthened. Strengthening a positive thought is a skill that can be developed.

Strengthening a positive thought is a five-step process:

<u>Step</u>: Recognize the positive thought as it comes to your mind. A positive thought is about *acceptance, progress, hope, optimism, meeting a standard, being good, being good at (anything), having the potential to achieve (anything positive).*

These thoughts begin with statements such as: *I am good.... I am good at.... I am improving, I can be... I am a good person, I am advancing in.... I am gaining.... I am making a valued contribution.... I have the potential to... I am equal.*

Example of recognizing a positive thought:

Allow yourself to become aware of a positive thought as it comes to mind.

Say hello to the positive thought such as, *I am good at being a Doctor, Nurse, Teacher, Manager, Craftsperson, Mother, Father, Student, Clerk, Fire Person, I recognize you.*

<u>Step</u>: Accept the positive thought.

An example statement of accepting a positive thought: *I recognize you as the positive thought - I am good at being a ...(title here).........and I accept you.*

<u>Step</u>: Announce to the positive thought that you are strengthening its positive nature. To strengthen a

positive thought you must simply define it with words of a stronger meaning.

Example of strengthening a positive thought:

Say to the positive thought, *I am strengthening your positive nature. I am changing your title from, "I am good at being .." a Doctor, Nurse, Teacher, Manager, Craftsperson, Mother, Father, Student, Clerk, Fire person. Your new title is, "I am one of the best of .." Doctors, Nurses, Teachers, Managers, Craftspersons, Mothers, Fathers, Students, Clerks, Fire-persons.*

Step: Declare that the thought has been changed to match the new title. Also, the new title is accurate and permanent until again changed by you.

Step: Acknowledge that this thought has changed to a stronger positive title. Example: *With the help of God, I accept this new, more positive title as permanent until I again change it.*

———

Note one: It is recommended that you do not change a positive thought to - *I am the best of (anything)...* Why? Because always striving to be the best of anything can create a high level of personal stress.

Note two: If you are one who is learning a craft or profession such as a journeyman, a student, an intern, etc., limit your positive thought to your current position. Examples: *I am one of the best students of history, I am one of the best of those who are learning this craft, I am one of the best interns in.......* While you are learning, it is rare that you will be one of the best of those who have studied and spent considerable time practicing your craft or profession.

Note three: It is recommended that you strengthen a positive thought to the level of *I am one of the best* only in areas where you have the given talent to be one of the best. You may have the talent to be one of the best teachers, but not the best of golfers.

———

About Positive Personal Declarations

Positive declarations stimulate new possibilities for succeeding in living well in life's changing cycles. New possibilities come through thinking in a broader set of categories.

Nine positive personal declarations for you to consider.

1. When I know the things I should do to live well, I do the things I should do to live well.

2. When I cherish what I am doing for another, life becomes cherish-able.

3. When I have a simple plan and seek the help I need, I gain confidence that I am in control of the situation.

4. Taking the time I need to foster my health is a necessary and uplifting gift to myself, to my family, to my friends, and to my community.

5. Free Will reigns. When I am listening to a person giving insistent advice, I accept it as a suggestion to consider. I listen to and consider the suggestions made by credible people.

6. Listening to credible suggestions helps me update my assumptions about succeeding in living well.

7. I am maturing and living well. I am contributing to the harmony in my family and community. I will accept the help offered to me by credible people in my family and community.

8. I give consideration to the suggestions of my family, my friends, and community members when I am making major decisions. I involve them to assure my decisions are well balanced.

9. I enjoy spending time to be with people who enjoy being with me.

_____

About the Value of Positive Beliefs

Believing that life is eternal can have a powerfully positive effect on our ability to deal with dramatic losses in our lives.

The poem, Imagine - background circumstances

Our daughter, Cynthia Jean, died at age 19 in an automobile accident on March 23, 1985, while in college. On March 24th at about 2 A.M. I was awakened by my inner voice with the urge to write. I went downstairs and picked up a pen and paper; the words began to flow.

Daddy, she said, I am ecstatic. You must write my poem for my friends. It is called, Imagine.

My poem, Imagine

Imagine seeing God who creates flowers
Imagine being with God who created the world
Imagine seeing the beauty of God the Father
Imagine Jesus stepping out to greet me
Imagine all of your ancestors calling to say hello
Imagine grandma's eyes
Imagine my surprise
Imagine meeting grandpa for the first time
Imagine time no more
Imagine majesty beyond belief

Imagine seeing God's face
Imagine life with beauty so incredible
it dazzles your eyes
Imagine life with friends of all the ages
Imagine God is larger than the universe
Imagine me trying to put my arms 'round
Imagine me among the angels
Imagine the wine of the angels
Imagine lucky me
Imagine being among those who love you so
Imagine love without boundaries
Imagine light that warms
Imagine wind that is still
Imagine saying hello to guardians of trust,
hope and love
Imagine God knowing your thoughts,
your emotions, your needs
Imagine the delicacy of a rose
Imagine a guardian of beauty
Imagine seeing Mary, the most beautiful mother
in the universe
Imagine the tenderness of hands
recreating the world each day
Imagine God's life in each leaf, each blade, each person
Imagine being lifted and carried around Heaven
by those who are powerful and swift
Imagine a host of Angels that sing just right
Imagine not one frightening thing
Imagine time no more
Imagine Mommy hugging me

Imagine me in your arms
Imagine the sky blue
Imagine I am with you
Imagine sitting with God
to talk about what interests you
Imagine experiencing all of this
because God loves us

Love you, Cindy
©1985, John Patrick Gatton

———

Chapter Nine: Prayers to Consider on Occasion

1. Prayer of forgiving others

(Name) _____, for any thought, word, or action
of yours that may have hurt me, I forgive you. I forgive
you wholly, completely, absolutely, and without
reservation.

2. Prayer for forgiving myself

I forgive myself for any thought, word, or action of mine
that may have hurt others, or me. I forgive myself wholly,
completely, absolutely, and without reservation. I resolve
to treat myself and others well.

3. Prayers about being an involved participant in life

A. Today, God, I journey with You, in You, and through
You in unity and harmony with all of creation.

B. Hello Inner Peace, with you I am (healing, journeying,
giving care, celebrating, recovering, advancing,
becoming).

How do you feel?   A+

Chapter Ten - Casual Uplifting Messages

Love vs. Material Things

Material things look good and have good taste until they go out of style, or deteriorate in a natural way. In real life it is love that perpetually satisfies. Love is the verve of life and is always with us. Love creates new life, ignites laughter, happiness, healing, forward movement, and the joy achieved in living well.

_____

What Should I Observe?

Observe a touch of compassion, an indication of love shared, a bit of music, an answer of yes, recognition of the beautiful gifts in life, participation in the community, sharing happiness with friends, spontaneous laughter, a gift given with a smile. Observe a word of praise, one who is opening to love, a compassionate touch of a face, an approval of any good result, a sincere attempt, a test completed.

Observing goodness in ourselves and our neighbors sets the living environment of discovery and the expansion of joy among us.

Imagine! We observe goodness and find joy!

_____

A Remarkable View

Mother Earth is an expression of the Creator. It is a magnificent creation serving uncountable useful purposes.

Each person is created and integrated with all that exists. Each is of value to all that is created. Each person is an integrated life-filled being adding human gifts to the universe. Gifts that include love, happiness, joy, music, varied talents, laughter, attraction, celebration, and free-will to participate in harmonious behavior.

―――――

Each Creation Is an Encore

As each structure is created in the universe the pattern for each to follow now exists. The living person is an encore to the very first man and woman. Our limited qualities include free-will, the ability to share love, growth of all sorts, the sharing of gifts, humor that enhances happiness, and the desire to serve others. In sharing these natural qualities we contribute to the harmony of all creation.

―――――

Not One Frightening Thing

I saw Mary. She is spiritually beautiful, amazing, fully human, ordinary and breathtaking. Who has seen her? How did I know it was she?

I noticed love-filled eyes, a deeply relaxed nature, wordless conversation, untroubled presence, affirming vibrations of a loving person, release of my hesitating thoughts, friendship, resonating oneness, certainty, peacefulness, initial witness, freely shared love, acceptance, perfect love, total confidence, the presence of complete truth, and not one frightening thing.

———

The Value of Musical Sounds

Pluck the string of a guitar, listen to the vibrations created for you within your range of listening. Why are you able to hear and enjoy this charming sound? Open your mind to think of what God would do for those who are created.

What would the unlimited creator do for those created? One answer lies in this following question: *If you could create a sound that delighted your child, or any child, would you create that sound?*

———

The Neighborhood

The neighborhood is a place fostering life-giving relationships. Neighbors speak, smile, laugh, say hello, grieve, reach out exampling deep-felt positive ethical principles. Neighbors form the norms with which we live; beliefs and historical norms that shape neighborhood behavior.

A neighbor displays love by lifting the child and smiling at his presence. A neighbor chatting about today's life brings friendship. A neighbor brings a gift of celebration displaying shared happiness. Each act displaying kindness, caring, or the sharing of life, forms the mixture of neighboring experiences.

Neighbors are open to companionship, cheerfulness, welcoming, cheering, doing for, and remembering good things. These actions encourage exciting relationships and the encouraging support of enjoying life.

Historians speak of guiding principles. Neighbors create norms and the encouragement of living well. In neighborhoods one discovers the existence of love and the effects of acceptance, mutual respect, sharing daily life, forgiveness.

The neighborhood creates opportunities to discover the value of God's command to love your neighbor. These remarkable neighborhood influences stimulate mutual sharing of love in community life.

_____

Bee Friendly

To be Bee friendly, a Bee must learn how to dance, sing, move in concert with the colony's traditions. The dance of friendliness tells of the direction and distance to life-giving nectar. Body moves are well known gestures describing scents, tastes, sounds, sights, how something feels, where it is.

The Bee's song must identify turning points, sights to see, and turn-around markers. Words are not said, there is no need. A Bee cannot speak a command; it doesn't know how.

To be Bee friendly, one must know the colony's ways, the dances, the songs, the description of distance, the place of life-giving nectar and its quality. The Bee must know the process of hunting, retrieving, homing. To be Bee friendly a Bee must participate in building the colony.

To be human friendly one must know how to search, to reach out, to find, to be with, to stand ready, to display love, to help out, to assist, to seek positive views, to encourage proper turns, and when to rest.

Are these processes so different? Aren't the results alike? Don't the Bees buzz 'round to keep the colony healthy, well fed, perpetual? Don't we have the same purposes in sharing with our community as the Bees in their buzzing friendliness?

Eye Contact
A Grandparent's View

Each of six grandchildren looks into my eyes when talking to me. This eye contact transmits unspoken messages. Messages about the refreshment of shared love, confidence that I am important, love conveyed to me, knowledge of their intent, a sense of humor, the understanding of sadness,

A grandchild's eye contact also transmits insights into current emotions, vibrancy of personality, fermentation of self-confidence, awareness of important issues, mutual acceptance, observation of human complexities, and flowing love.

A grandchild's eyes transmit to me peacefulness, confirmation of the value of my listening, recognition given and received. Reflections of happiness within the family are contained in the simple act of looking directly into a grandchild's eyes.

Eye contact with my grandchildren brings the joy of realizing I am loved by two generations. One generation

I fathered. One generation I have nurtured as a member of an ancient family that dates back to Adam and Eve.

———

One Act of Kindness
Why is one act of kindness so important?

One act of kindness is a recognition of a need becoming apparent, an observation made, a thought coming forth. Then, a gift given such as a word of comfort, an extended hand holding a coin for supper, a ride home, an overnight stay, a cup of soup, a word of happiness, recognition of mutual humanness, empathy.

Kindness is a surprisingly uplifting gift - a kiss on the cheek, a healing touch, a show of light, a ray of hope, tuition paid, a night without fear, a day of sun, a cold drink at noon, a sandwich purchased, a bowl of beans, a chicken dinner, a cart for hauling, a message of acceptance.

And so the cycle goes - once again a kind act is observed, then the gifting is noticed, a memory is formed. So it continues day and night until each of us observes a need, then reaches out to another created one; thus perpetuating the effects of shared love flowing to each created being, each entity.

———

How do you feel?   A+

Chapter Eleven
Addenda

These additional ideas, stories, learning processes, and readings provide innovative ways to encourage reflections that stimulate the brain and create lively discussions.

First Addendum

In this first addendum you will find motivational and brain stimulating stories, processes, and suggestions that inspire the sharing of insights and wisdom through mutual discussions.

———

An essay
Some Benefits of Group Discussions

One objective of mutual group discussions about tools for lifelong learning is - *To help group participants become aware that these tools are available.*

The discussion group becomes a mutual learning center. Listening skills develop as each person becomes a teacher as well as an inquisitive student. Because we gain wisdom over the years the subject discussed in any meeting may be familiar. However, because we advance in experience and view the subject differently, the content of each discussion can be quite different. Participants discover how the discussion applies to themselves. In this process each of us is learning how to improve our skills in living well.

———

A story to stimulate discussion
Different Signals

Signals indicate feelings, directions and other stuff. Mr. Body is sending me lots of new signals these days, messages like, slow down, reach out to help, speak up, refuse high-challenge assignments, take care of this or that part of me, enjoy the day, re-imagine success.

Signals indicate I should tell it like it is, prepare the way, simplify, get up, speak of positive stuff, talk about life's events with friends, go with others to have some fun, go for a bike ride when I feel run-down.

I hear these messages, or maybe I feel them as they present themselves in the advancing cycles of my life. A positive thought uplifts and urges me to reconsider how to live well through these persistently changing signals and their meanings.

Perhaps my sister explained the cycles signals and their meanings best when she said two weeks before she passed. *Well, brother, life has been good for me, I know Heaven is a good place to be, and, when I arrive there, my husband, the love of my life, will also greet me.*

Perhaps these signals are a part of evolving cycles bringing new understanding of what life is about. It seems to me that the persistent enjoyment of life is one of the great lessons that prepare me for upcoming events.

———

Learning Opportunity:
Creating and Sustaining a Positive Living Environment

The purpose of this three part learning opportunity is to help discussion leaders develop a concise common language for discussing how to create and sustain a positive living environment.

———

Daily decisions made by group members influence the living environment of the group. A positive living environment promotes the enjoyment of being an exploring group member.

———

Learning Opportunity:
Consider and discuss each item in the following three part review of selected qualities, actions, and results of building and sustaining a positive living environment.

1. Extending the listed qualities of a positive living environment:

• Each person is accepted as a member of the group.
• Structured and random acts of kindness occur.
• Respect is shown for different traditions held by group members.
• Mutual positive goals exist and compromises are made for living in harmony with group members.

- Responsible and positive contributions are made by group participants.
- Each member recognizes the value of mutual respect shown by group members.
- Members enjoy their experiences associated with being a member of a group.
- The existence of positive relationships is frequently recognized.
- Group members identify what they have in common.
- Persistent recalling of the benefits created by focusing on what the members have in common.

2. Examples of activities associated with a positive living environment:

- Each group member is considered to be equally important to the achievement of a positive group living environment.
- Small acts of kindness are practiced formally and randomly.
- Relaxed inquiries about each person's life stories, beliefs, and traditions are made and considered to be polite inquiries.
- Individuals review their own assumptions to determine the influence their assumptions are having on their own behavior as a group member.
- Statements that seem to be challenges to one's assumptions are interpreted as suggestions; not as commands or insults.
- Compromises are discussed, negotiated, and made.

• Actions that promote harmony among members of the group are celebrated. An example is, saying thanks to the other group members for sharing life stories.
• Sincere individual expressions about the value of the group discussions are made.
• Celebration of the harmony among members of the group is continual.
• Continual inquiry and discovery of activities that promote harmony, acceptance, good health, happiness, joy in life, and peace in daily life.

3. A short list of results occurring within a positive living environment:

• Mutual discussions allow participants to share wisdom.
• The traditions and life stories of other group members become familiar.
• The value of respecting the traditions of other group members is learned.
• Good news is frequently shared.
• Acts of kindnesses ranging from opening a door to delivering meals are frequent.
• Saying thanks for those acts of kindness is a frequent act of kindness.
• Individual's feeling of being a respected member of a group are supported.
• Individuals accept responsibility to contribute to positive goals and harmony among group members.

———

Learning Opportunity:
Becoming Aware of Our Listening Habits

Is What I Hear the Same as What Was Said?

I can repeat the message in the words said if what I hear is the same as what was said. An example: What was said was, *I think birds are an important part of our environment.*

If I interpret the message rather than simply record it, I say what I interpreted when asked what was actually said. This creates a communications problem. What I interpreted may be the result of my own prejudices. Example: what was actually said - *I think birds are an important part of our environment.* What I interpreted was, *This person wants to talk about birds until I fall asleep.*

Why is this piece of knowledge important? When I share stories about life events, I tell those stories and listen to the stories others tell me. If I follow the natural tendency of interpreting the messages I hear, rather than mentally recording those messages, I have become a prejudiced listener. As a result of trusting my interpretation of a story, I ask questions that send the signal that I am not listening, I am judging. I was not recording what the person told me about his or her life events. I was interpreting their meaning.

Sharing stories about our life events is an important aspect of building trust between people. The development of trust is a goal of the process of sharing life with people. Sharing our lives with others is an inspiring, bonding experience.

What is the skill involved in becoming a listener who encourages the sharing of life stories and, therefore, the sharing of life? The skill of listening involves being aware that you are interpreting as the person speaks; then stopping the act of interpreting and focusing on mentally recording what is actually being said.

———

Note: Suggestions for redeveloping the skill of mentally recording what actually was said include: when you hear yourself saying to someone, *What you seem to be saying is ...*

OR,

I have the feeling that what you are saying is ... recognize that you are speaking about an interpretation you made about what the person actually said.

Once you recognize you are speaking of your interpretation, decide not to give that interpretation. In future conversations focus on listening and mentally recording what is actually said. Then ask further questions that respond to what was actually said.

———

Learning Opportunity
An essay

About how Wisdom Develops as We Mature

During each maturing year of life experiences, the opportunity to expand our personal wisdom exists. Our memories and our frame of reference become deeper, broader. Our insights are changing each day. Those insights are about the process of taking action, observing consequences, gaining knowledge, deciding what action to take, taking a new action or not changing.

We continually learn, gain knowledge and gather insights about how to steer our lives to achieve success as we define success. That is one reason the wisdom of more mature persons is often full of suggestions that lead to success. Wisdom is the quality of having experience, knowledge and good judgement based on principles of how to successfully share life with others.

Success in life is defined by each of us. Some folks define success by using general categories such as the following - *the sharing of love, being loved, accepting others and being accepted, honoring others and accepting their honoring of our positive contributions to harmony among us. It also includes the category of accepting the needed assistance of others while we experience life's challenging events.*

The cycle of learning and adjusting to life is reason enough for each of us to listen to those with substantial years of experience. The elements of the learning cycle include - *taking action, observing the results, studying newly available information and techniques, changing behavior, observing the consequences, and again deciding what action to take in similar events. This cycle repeats continually.*

———

Learning Opportunity:
The following four part thesis is written to stimulate group discussion about the value of wisdom developed during our life experiences. This discussion stimulates the brain and generates fascinating insights about an elder's continuing value to family, neighbors, and community as we add the wisdom developed in our more mature years.

———

A thesis
We Are the Sages

Part one

We are not the matured, we are maturing. We are the Sages who have sculpted lessons, decisions, responsibilities, observations, and consequences into wisdom.

In our maturing, we have become Sages. We have
learned and discerned things like - *the expression of
love, the value of praise, the importance of thanksgiving,
the results of observing goodness, the contribution
made to individuals by listening to their stories.*

As Sages we have - no *boundaries, no rules, no
obligations without consent, no directives, no imposed
routines, no signals of which path to take. There are no
signs saying don't leap ahead. Deep-water swimming is
allowed.*

Sponsoring others is rewarding. Observing the grace,
speed, purpose, and silence in nature is satisfying. Excitement comes with reaching out to help.
Absolute truths have diminished, reality is shaped by
experiences of love, friendship, consequences.

Part two

We are free of the claims of others, loaded with curiosity,
open to learning, wanderers in the world we explore. We
feel the vibrations of life, the whisperings of those who
have passed. We long to be with creation, created
things, creative beings.

We have learned to express joy, to relish the vibrations
of touch, to recognize radiant energy within a neighbor's
caring. We have learned to avoid sapping conflict. We
have learned the value of forgiveness, the harmony

created by a smile, the importance of sharing wisdom, the sharing of happiness inherent in a youngster's thanksgiving.

In our maturing we have become Sages. We are active creators. We are communicators of how to, when to, where to. We have learned to say I forgive you, I enjoy you, I respect you.

We are the broadcasters of happiness in life. We encourage knowing who we really are.

Part three

We are the teachers of how to read road signs, the wise navigators in the shifting winds of life, the captains of altered destinies, the matrons and patrons of mercy, the providers caring about the needy.

We are armored by the results of life's trials, softened by love, redirected by serving others, knowers of how to win and how to learn from losing. We are the Sages, those with life's wisdom, the ones who predict with some accuracy. We are those who know how to avoid, how to interweave, how to recreate positive goals.

We steer in catastrophic winds. We paddle when dog-tired. We give hugs while half asleep. We tranquilize with adroit touch. We reassure with an insightful phrase.

We slam the door on inequality. We walk safely through emotional storms. We reach and give a dollar from nearly empty pockets.

We speak of how to enjoy life, mingle academia with experience, provide responsible and honest leadership. We speak to encourage success, to uplift thoughts that create dreams. We know how to visualize success in spite of our flaws.

Part four

We are the Elders, now the Sages. We compel listening through dispensing subtle wisdom. We are guardians of social justice. We are guides to new generations. We are the qualified advisers, mentors, diplomats, thinkers, intellectuals. We are the skilled craft-persons, the scholars, matured mystics, gurus, wizards of how to.

We are the Sages. Come, gather 'round for we are parents, teachers, lovers, family promoters, those who have learned through exciting living, those who savor life, and those who foster the evolution of humanness.

Suggested Subjects for Future Discussions

- Uplifting messages, humor and laughter, changing how we feel
- Commonly known indicators of living well

- How to change negative thoughts
- How to strengthen positive thoughts
- Experiencing the effects of relaxation exercises
- Recognizing how assumptions and expectations influence our wellness
- Sharing the fun of life with neighbors
- The value of baking muffins for a friend

———

Guidelines for Maintaining Mutual Discussions

Following is an example handout at the beginning of the first meeting of a group.

The goal of this series of mutual discussions is to provide participants with the opportunity to mutually consider various ways to think about living well. The facilitator's responsibility is limited to administration and facilitating discussion. In brief, together, we are stimulating and broadening our thinking about living life well and sharing our insights and wisdom that come from years of learning and accumulating knowledge through life experiences.

As a participant in these mutual discussions, please read the following guidelines for getting the most from the conversations designed to help us mutually discuss different ways of thinking about how to succeed.

1. All materials presented and all statements made are only suggestions for you to consider.
2. Raise nothing that is said in meetings, or is printed in this book, above the level of a suggestion for your consideration.
3. As a participant, avoid using words such as - *you must; you have to; there is only one way to ___ ; that is not true; I recommend.*
4. If words or phrases such as those presented above (in # 3) are said, interpret them as suggestions, not as recommendations or commands. This action can help each of us stay relaxed while exploring suggestions presented. It is suggested that each of us listen with the objective of learning about other participants, the stories of their lives, and the insights and wisdom they have gained while living life's events.
5. This is not a course for a thorough study of the subject. It is a set of stimulating discussion meetings to offer initial information and simple methods to encourage further reading, life enhancing skills development, and the sharing of information and wisdom.
6. All conversations and discussions during this series are about how we are doing and what we could do to succeed in living well. Since these are discovery and review sessions they are considered private to the members of this discussion group.
7. There probably will not be enough time to complete all of the activities suggested for any one session. After the meeting is complete, you may want to

continue discussing these activities with others who are also attending the session.

Note: The tools offered for your consideration during these sessions about living well are stimulating enough to be discussed during an entire lifetime. They can be rich subjects for continuing discussions in groups, your neighborhood, and in community meetings.

––––––

Helpful Examples for Discussion Leaders

Invitation/Announcement
A suggested note of introduction

We are planning to start a series of discussions about tools and skills for living well and you are invited to be a participant in this discussion group. Groups will be limited to fifteen participants.

Meetings about living well center on the tools and skills for succeeding. They are about viewing life and experiencing life in uplifting ways as we mature; also, sharing our insights and successes about living well. One objective of these mutual discussions is to look at life in uplifting ways and consider many paths of how to live well.

This Living Well series of mutual discussions is facilitated by an experienced person with the goal of helping individuals succeed in living well in each cycle of life.

Subjects of the mutual discussions include:

1. Uplifting messages, humor and laughter, changing how we feel
2. Commonly known indicators of living well
3. How to change negative thoughts
4. How to strengthen positive thoughts
5. Experiencing the effects of relaxation exercises
6. Recognizing how assumptions and expectations influence our wellness
7. Sharing the fun of life with friends and neighbors

_____

An Example Process for Meeting One
Subjects Include:
1. Examining Selected Indicators of Living Well
2. About Laughter and Humor
3. How Wisdom Develops

_____

Use the following theories to stimulate discussion about how wisdom develops:

How wisdom develops, a theory

Wisdom develops as we mature, become experienced, observe, make decisions, live with the consequences of our decisions, take responsibility, change direction to adjust to different conditions. Again we experience consequences of those adjustments, acquire knowledge, and add insights to our memories.

———

How wisdom is shared, a theory

Wisdom is shared in many ways including informal chats, research papers, daily suggestions, parental comments, classroom discussions, body language, silence, and a multitude of other ordinary activities.

———

Discuss and demonstrate how laughter changes our feelings.

10 minute activity: Use the following five step process to lead the group in practicing how to feel better by simply smiling and laughing.

1. Register how you feel now.
2. Touch your fingers to the muscles of your cheek bones .
3. Raise those muscles until your face shows a broad smile.
4. How do you feel now?
5. What influence does your smile have on how your neighbor feels?
20 minute activity:

1. Let's laugh together continuously for 15 seconds.
2. Discuss how do you feel now?
3. What reactions did you have to this exercise?
4. Have participants tell stories, and quips that create laughter.

Discuss the fourteen indicators of living well on page thirteen.

Read aloud the fourteen Indicators of living well. Then, discuss the selected indicators and how they apply in our daily activities.

Meeting two will be about:
1. Recognizing physical stress and associated relaxation techniques.
2. About the motivational effects of being equal
3. Recognizing the influence of our assumptions.

––––––

An Example Process for Meeting Two

This meeting is about how our assumptions influence our success in living well and how changing an assumption can change a life.

1. Ten minute activity: Review page 19 for Recognizing Physical Stress.

2. Thirty minute activity: Becoming aware of our
   assumptions and our equality with others.

Reminder: Mutual discussion among equals is the
essential method of our exploring and expanding our
potential success in living well.

Definition of the word, assumption: anything that is
accepted as true, or as certain to happen, without proof.
Examples are: *Belief; Expectation; Conjecture;
Speculation; Guess.*

Synonyms of the word, assumption, include - *a thought,
an expectation, a speculation, a belief, a supposition, a
guess, a surmise, a premise.*

Definition of a Fact: Something that is accepted as true
and unchanging.

_____

Learning Opportunity:
Is the following statement an assumption, or is it a fact?
When we *think of ourselves as equal to other people we
are inclined to reach out and engage with positive
people and engage in healthy activities.*

Has your experience shown that the above statement is
a fact? ___ yes ___ no

Lead a discussion as follows:

1. Ask one participant to read the story titled, *Equality*.
2. Discuss the assumptions the author has expressed in the writing titled, *Equality*. Discuss any agreement or disagreement with the author's assumptions.
3. Read and discuss the assumptions that the author has expressed in the writing titled, *About the Value Being Equal*. See page 22-23.

Discuss any agreement or disagreement with the author's assumptions.

Note: Meeting three will be about having a purpose in life.

_____

An Example Process for Meeting Three

This meeting is about having a purpose in life

1. Introduction.

Definition: A Purpose is commonly defined as an intention or an objective. Declaring a purpose creates highly motivational statements that support our focus on positive goals.

Positive purposes in life can include - h*aving fun, helping others, being with friends, healthy living, gaining knowledge, advancing in a career, caring for a family, education, skills development.*

Thirty minute discussion:
1. Make an informal list of eight common positive purposes in life.
2. Have you explored the current purpose, or purposes, in your life?
3. If you were to declare a different current purpose, or purposes in life, would your future plans and activities be different?

Stating a purpose in life creates a motivational statement that triggers positive decisions leading to success in living well.

A common definition of the word, motivational: promoting the willingness to achieve something.

Learning Opportunity:
Discuss and answer the following two questions.
1. What is a positive primary purpose that you have in your life? Page 27
2. What is a secondary purpose that you have in your life?

General discussion of the value of having a purpose in life. Participants tell of the purposes in life they declare for themselves.

Thirty Minute discussion:
About creating new possibilities for living well

1. A possibility for living life well comes into existence when we examine and change restrictive assumptions about the possibility of succeeding in living well.
2. Group Discussion: Is succeeding in living well in life's changing cycles the result of a decision, or set of decisions, or is it the result of circumstances?

Note: Meeting four will be about common issues we face as we mature, and creating new possibilities.

———

An Example Process for Meeting Four

About common issues in life as we mature; and about creating new possibilities

Background Information: Four commonly known categories of issues we face as maturing adults are, *losses, major external changes of most any type, physical changes, and emotional changes.*

1. Mutually discuss, explore, and add to this list of issues experienced while we mature:
A. Losses
B. Emotional changes
C. External changes
D. Physical Changes

2. Discuss the following questions:
A. How do our assumptions influence our decisions?

B. If we wanted to update one of our assumptions, is it possible?

_____

More Uplifting Stories to Stimulate Discussion

The Beauty of a Flower

The budding flower attracts my eyes, raises curiosity within me. The opening flower attracts my noticing. The open flower pulls my face to it like gravity.

Closeness to a flower expands my desire to observe perfection, opens my noticing of scents, flares my nostrils, opens the observing pupils of my eyes, stimulates my memory cells in hope of instant recall, magnifies created details so I may recognize miniaturization achieved.

Attention to a flower brings delicate stems into glorious focus, registers buds popping from delicate weight-bearing stems, notes mature beauty within minute blossoms, it arouses and records appreciation of unique leaves, of well matched colors, it commemorates mind penetrating scents, stores the love emoting images stimulated by such beauty.

Nearness of a flower awakens my brain patterns to an infinite creator, fashions harmony within my body's systems, extends happiness to each cell, heals disturbed emotions, calms my muscles, soothes my nerves, relaxes my eyes.

Memories of a flower lift my facial muscles into a smile that spreads happiness to nearby faces, thus promoting my awareness of the purpose of blossoming beauty occurring within the cycles of my lifetime.

___

There Are more Flowers than Doubts

I count the doubts that trundle about in my brain and regret their presence. I shoo them away with confidence and change their nature to more pleasant thoughts; then, other doubts roll rapidly in.

It is like being inside a bee hive, and, yet, I seem to win. Eventually, my energy becomes stronger because I am open to unceasing love.

In the times of flooding doubts, I count nearby flowers created from the presence of ceaseless love. So, the cycle goes like this - doubts trundle about in my brain like raindrops, I shoo them out, I change their nature and focus attention on nearby flowers attracting my complete being.

I count the miniature stems within the flowers and their blossoms that seem weightless. Their scent wafts through my senses, calms my mind, relaxes my tendency to accept doubt as the nuances of color shadings engage my mind in wonderment, transforming those doubts into deeper appreciation of creation.

___

Beauty Is Irresistible

Love is the source of life, beauty, happiness, joy,
positive choices, the motivation to contribute.

Why share love? you asked. Love stimulates the
person, the plant, the animal, life in the world.
Stimulating love sparks life, caring, sharing, touching,
positive response, desire to serve, serving, healing,
pregnancy in every positive aspect of it.

Why is the blossoming of beauty irresistible? you asked.
Because beauty is created through the sharing of love.
Why is mature beauty irresistible? you asked. It is the
result of the gift of life, deciding, caring, sharing,
touching, positive response, serving, healing, and
pregnant giving.

———

How do you feel?   A+ 🙂

More Techniques for Stimulating Discussion

Exploring a Vision Statement

Learning Opportunity:
Examine the following statements and begin discussions
to develop a mission statement with longer term goals
and daily objectives for this discussion group.

Purpose: Discussing a vision statement for the group
stimulates us to dwell on identifying positive meanings of
life, positive longer term goals, and daily activities that
affect how we feel. Reflecting on these meanings helps
us to know how we can contribute to harmony in the
family, in social groups, and in our communities.

Note: Promoting lively discussions is the goal. Writing
perfect vision statement is not the goal.

_____

Vision Statements to Stimulate Discussion
Our vision statement could be:

To continually search for, and discover truths, pathways,
processes, and perceptions that enable us to adjust to
changing life situations and participate in our own
achievement of success as we define it.

— OR —

The following could be our vision statement: We live life
as though it were a dance with changing rhythms. We

encourage others to join in the fun of life. We laugh and we notice that you feel better. We experience the joy of being productive at what we want to do. We forgive, and therefore, we are happier

———

Defining Success for Ourselves

Learning Opportunity:
Read and discuss the following statement and question.

1. Success for me is continually feeling that I am living life well within life's natural and changing cycles.

2. Should our goals in living well include the following - to *sustain happiness, joyfulness, exhilaration, delight, pleasure, excitement, peacefulness, and an occasional thrill while living life's events?*

Learning Opportunity:
Review and discuss the following listed daily objectives; also, add your objectives:

1. To use and share wisdom that accumulates through ever-changing situations.
2. To enjoy daily life by continually enabling ourselves to adjust to life cycles.
3. To have a briefly stated plan for the future.
4. To continually reassess our assumptions.

5. To recognize others as important sharers of life and community.
6. (add your objectives)

——————

Potential Future Discussion Topics
Give priority to these subjects:
1. __Discovering truth and deciding which truths serve me well.
2. __Telling my life stories and listening to the stories others tell about life experiences.
3. __ Sharing life with others each day, thereby contributing to the well-being of others.
4. __ Accepting the help that I need.
5. __ Re-visualizing success in the current time periods.
6. __ Learning how to enhance our feeling of wellness.
7. __ What makes us feel joyful?
8. __ How does expecting success affect our daily activities?
9. __ How does recognizing my value to my family and community affect how I feel?
10. __ How does feeling that I am important to other people affect my activities?
11. __ How are my activities affected by - sharing love, honoring others for what they do, and being honored for the good things I do?
12. __ Does laughing affect my health?
13. __ How does one contribute to the harmony within family and community?

14. __ Let's talk about a variety of proven ways to relax; also, let's talk about using them.

15. __ Why is being entertained and entertaining others important to me?

16. __ What activities do we do that promote our mental, physical, emotional, and spiritual health?

17. __ How does living in sync with my accepted beliefs affect my ability to succeed in adjusting to life's changing cycles?

18. (add yours)

———

Creating Daily Guidelines for Succeeding

Simple, very specific daily activities do enhance our success in living well

Learning Opportunity:
Read, discuss, and add to the following suggestions for daily guidelines for succeeding:

1. Know the name of the person who provides services for you.

2. In some way, reward those who serve you in any way.

3. Help anyone who is in distress.

4. Every obstacle presents an opportunity to improve our living environment.

5. Give so that others may live well.

6. Make a briefly stated plan for the future.

7. Create an uplifting objective for today.

8. Promote the discovery of truth, new pathways, and processes for success in living well.

9. Treat each person as an important contributor to harmony among us.

10. (your additional guidelines)

_____

Three Quoted Testimonies
from participants in these discussions

1. Success in living well is a cooperative effort.
2. We decided to come to our next meeting with brief statements about how each of us is already trying to live well. In the process, we started to reveal our personal feelings only to realize that we had already accepted a sense of group trust which, in and of itself, was a remarkably good feeling. Living life well is a cooperative effort yielding the highest of warm feelings in the process.
3. We listen to understand, to accept, and to appreciate the people in the group and their suggestions. That is what we are trying to do in our meetings and it is a joy to experience.

_____

The following are answers that group participants gave to the following question - _Why are our living well group discussions special and satisfying?_

1. Acceptance - each person is accepted as important to each other person.
2. We are opening to new thoughts by listening to hear what is said while forgoing judgements and considering what the other person's suggestion could mean to me.
3. We are willing to learn from the stories about life that others tell: that is, accepting each person as having well-earned wisdom and credibility. Each person has learned, decided what to do, examined results, examined personal assumptions, and adjusted personal behavior based on the lessons learned while living those experiences.
4. We express gratitude for contributions made by group members to help us improve our ability to discern, learn, and consider changing personal behavior to achieve success. We are grateful for the wisdom others share about how to adjust to ever-changing life situations.

Second Addendum: The Value of Remembering

Three Ancient Biblical Quotes

Purpose: Modern day research and the development of knowledge about human behavior is vitally important to our human development. It is important to continually integrate newly developing and reliable knowledge into our thinking about how to live well. Ancient writings also contain many valuable lessons about Living Well. Three

quotes from ancient sources follow. Two are from the
Old Testament and one from the New Testament.

———

Ancient quotes related to being equal

From the Old Testament: Book of Wisdom Chapter 7:1-6

Solomon Is Like All Other Men
I too am a mortal man, the same as all the rest and a
descendent of the first man of earth. And in my mother's
womb I was molded into flesh in a ten months' period,
body and blood, from the seed of man, and the pleasure
that accompanies marriage. And I too, when born,
inhaled the common air, and fell upon the kindred earth,
wailing; I uttered that first sound common to all. In
swaddling clothes and with constant care I was nurtured.
For no king has any different origin or birth, but one is
the entry into life for all; and in one same way they leave
it.

———

An Ancient Quote related to the timing of a suggestion.
From: Book of Sirach 20:19

A proverb when spoken by a fool is unwelcome, for he
does not utter it at the proper time.

———

An ancient quote about our relationship with others

From: New Testament, Mathew 7:12

The Golden Rule: Treat others the way you would have them treat you; this sums up the law and its prophets.

———

An essay
Sharing Love, One Purpose in Life

God is perfect love. Perfect love is the Creator, the Source of Life. Perfect love is trustable, always. Creation expands and adjusts to accept each newly created person. Therefore, creation adjusted to receive and accommodate you in your conception. Your mother felt that adjustment.

Sharing love creates harmony among people and is an essential element of a positive living environment. Sharing love encourages positive thoughts about each person's value. This includes how I think of myself, my self-esteem.

Love expands to other persons when it is shared with free-will. Each person naturally desires the love of others, and each can be a part of the streaming of love. In free-will, love flows through each created life to other created lives. Each person participating in the flow of love is one important positive resource of a positive living environment for family, social groups, and for the larger community.

Each person has both a place and a purpose. The purpose of each person can be recognized through gifted intuitive inquiry, and by broadening one's life experiences.

Each person is capable of contributing to the harmony of a family, social groups, and their community. Each acknowledgement by any person of the value of any other person contributes to the harmony within a positive living environment. As love is shared, the harmony among us strengthens and expands.

Perfect Love is the source of life. It is also the source of positive visions, a positive state of being, inner peace, social growth, positive participation, and the sharing of one's life by serving others. Therefore, each person is capable of contributing to harmonious living in the family, in social groups, and in their community. A positive living environment is created through the sharing of love. Therefore, accepting love and sharing the love received become one single and positive purpose in life.

———

A Confirming Letter to My Grandchild

Dear Grandchild,

Your life's story began at home where, with family, you are learning that you are loved and you are part of a family. Your are learning that God has been the Creator of life for billions of years. You are observing that your sharing of love promotes harmony among us. Your smile causes the eyes of others to shine.

You are learning that yesterday's self discipline has positive effects on tomorrow's joy. You have noticed that creativity promotes forward movement, and freedom is earned by each generation.

You are observing that recognizing God in our lives enables us to harbor and think refreshingly healthy thoughts. Health promoting, refreshing thoughts bring new positive meanings to life's natural cycles.

———

In our Christian community you are learning that as we live life with God, through God, and in God, we attain an ever-increasing love of life, an ever-growing desire to serve. And, you are learning to accept perfect love.

Our community teaches that in being one with God we gain the knowledge that good deeds are honored, always, forever. We experience that God's acceptance of us is always perfect.

In our Christian community you are experiencing and observing that we are imperfect seekers of oneness with God. And you are becoming aware that even in our imperfection we are completely accepted as we are within the current cycle of life.

How do you feel?   A+

———-

A reflection
Positive Traditions Are Important

Years have passed as we have watched our children grow. We know their friends and acquaintances. Some have taken separate paths; some are lifetime friends.

It seems to me there are many similarities in the patterns of how our children live life and those related patterns in our lives. Our children greatly value friends. Children are like magnets in their lives. World events hold their interest. They show love for Mother Earth. They gather in bunches and celebrate the day.

Now, our children observe their own children. They lift a glass in joy and memory. They celebrate a break from tough times. They help their friends. They travel to visit family to encourage tightly knit relationships so their children will know the source of the values they hold.

I suppose our parents made similar observations. I hope our parents observed those same healthy trends during our own maturing life experiences. However, if they hadn't noticed those healthy trends, would we see them in our children, and in their children?

Tidbits of Wisdom for Sustaining Traditions
of Living Well

Traditions of living well are exampled in family life and activities, in our friendships, and in community activities.

Following are twenty-one selected tidbits of wisdom that have been shared by hundreds of people in seminars and retreats I have led during the past forty-two years. It is gratifying to now share and suggest that you review these tidbits of wisdom that can stimulate positive thinking and mutual discussion.

1. Don't be fooled by those who want you to play the fool.
2. Trust those of goodness who are like those your parents trusted.
3. Marry one who wants you to be a friend of God.
4. Marry one through whom goodness flows.
5. Keep company with folks whose thoughts, words and deeds, when integrated with yours, create harmony in your relationship.
6. Share love with those who are out-of-synch with the harmony created by sharing love.
7. Know the needs of those in need.
8. Keep company with those who help others.
9. Encourage those who can help, to help.
10. Know that we are influenced by our observations of daily behavior.
11. Know that we all share humanity.

12. Know that your behavior influences everyone you meet.

13. Know that everyone you influence influences all who share humanity.

14. Reach out to those who fall by their own willing or by things that just happen.

15. Assist those who cannot discern which choice is right.

16. If you say you speak for God, speak of love.

17. Think and act as though judging others is self-defeating.

18. Know that current behavior becomes a trend.

19. Understand that self-condemnation is self-destruction.

20. Know that we live to be with an unlimited God.

21. Know that joy is one result of sharing love.

JPG

Tracking Our Progress

Tracking Our Progress

Suggestions for stimulating a review of progress in the use of the tools for lifelong learning about living well.

In a group's first meeting use this set of questions to provide an overview of the content included in the discussions about living well and enjoying life.

Use the following set of questions on occasion to track your development of knowledge, familiarity with the tools for living well, and your skills development in the use of those tools.

1. How do you feel now about your use of the listed Guidelines for Maintaining Relaxed Mutual Discussions?

  A+

Book page: First addendum page 79

2. How do you feel now about the value of the information contained in the essay titled, About Living Well?

  A+

Book page 6

3. How do you feel now about your knowledge of the listing of Eight Qualities of A Motivational Living Environment?

  A+

Book page 7

4. How do you feel now about the usefulness of considering your current responses to the selected Fourteen Indicators of Living Well?

  A+

Book page 9

5. How do you feel now about the effects that, Uplifting Messages And Humor, have on you?

  A+ .

Book page 15

6. How do you feel now about the suggestion that you are equal to all other persons?

  A+

Book page 25

7. How do you feel now about your current declaration of a purpose in your life?

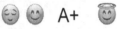 A+

Book page 27

8. How do you feel now about the value of uplifting stories shared in your group meetings?

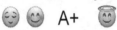 A+

9. How do you feel now about your ability to enhance your enjoyment of life by using the tool, Updating Our Assumptions?

 A+

Book page 30

10. How do you feel now about the possibility that you can succeed in living well?

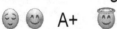 A+

11. How do you feel now about the relaxing effects resulting from your use of either of the tools, Meditation or Contemplation?

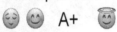 A+

Book page 37

12. How do you feel now about the effects your use of the tool, Changing a Negative Thought to a Positive Thought, have on your enjoyment of life?

  A+

Book page 44

13. How do you feel now about the effects your use of the tool, Strengthening a Positive Thought, have on your enjoyment of life?

  A+

Book page 48

14. How do you feel now about your ability to develop new possibilities by considering the Nine Positive Declarations presented in the book?

  A+

Book page 51

15. How do you feel now about the Value of Having Positive Beliefs?

  A+

Book page 53

16. How do you feel now about using the three, Prayers to Consider on Occasion, to help you feel better?

  A+

Book page 56

17. How do you feel now about the value of the content of the essay, Some Benefits of Group Discussions?

  A+

Book First Addendum page 67

18. How do you feel now about your knowledge of the content of the essay, Creating and Sustaining a Positive Living Environment?

  A+

Book First Addendum page 69

19. How do you feel now about the progress you have made in recording what someone said vs. trusting your interpretations of what the person said?

 A+

Book First Addendum page 72

20. How do feel now about the value you gained in your group's discussion about Exploring A Vision Statement?

  A+

Book First Addendum pages 95

21. How do you feel now about the accuracy of the following statement? We are building our positive living skills in our discussions about the tools for lifelong learning about living well.

  A+

22. How do you feel now about your own current declaration of what success in living well means to you?

  A+

Book First Addendum pages 96

23. How do you feel now about your ability to recognize physical stress within you?

  A+

Book page 19

24. How do you feel now about your ability to use the listed relaxation methods for reducing the physical stress that you now recognize?

  A+

Book page 20

25. How do you feel now about your knowledge of how to create Guidelines for Succeeding in living well?

 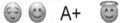 A+

Book First Addendum page 99

INDEX

My Notes About Living Well:

My Notes About Living Well:

Made in the USA
Lexington, KY
26 September 2018